INDO-UZBEK RELATIONS

PAST, PRESENT AND FUTURE

Suranjan Das

KNOWLEDGE WORLD
KW Publishers Pvt Ltd
New Delhi

The Court of Directors of the East India Company sent a despatch in July, 1854 to the Governor-General of India in Council, suggesting the establishment of the Universities of Calcutta, Madras and Bombay.

In pursuance of that despatch, the University of Calcutta was founded on January 24, 1857.

The University adopted in the first instance, the pattern of the University of London and gradually introduced modifications in its constitution.

ISBN 978-93-80502-76-2

KNOWLEDGE WORLD

Published in India by

Kalpana Shukla
KW Publishers Pvt Ltd
4676/21, First Floor, Ansari Road, Daryaganj, New Delhi 110002
Phone: +91.11.23263498 / 43528107
email: mail@kwpub.in / knowledgeworld@vsnl.net

Printed and Bound in India

CONTENTS

INDO-UZBEK RELATIONS— PAST, PRESENT, AND FUTURE[1]

India has been so historically linked with Central Asia that the region is known in Indian diplomatic parlance as its 'extended neighbour' or an 'immediate and strategic neighbourhood'. In this paradigm Uzbekistan, sharing a common boundary with other Central Asian Republics of Kazakhstan, Kyrgyzstan, Tajikistan, and Turkmenistan, occupies a crucial place. What I propose to do in the next few pages is to present the dynamics of Indo-Uzbek relations in the context of past, present, and future.

The Legacy

India and Central Asia are bound with each other by centuries of shared historical linkages. The Aryans reportedly migrated from the steppes of Eurasia to the plains of India. Archaeological excavations in north-west India and Central Asia have demonstrated close ties between India and Central Asia in terms of communities, settlements, economic, social, and cultural interactions during the ancient period. Buddhism spread to Central Asia from India during the Kushana period, and the significant presence of Buddhist centres and temples in Central Asia indicate the Buddhist impact in the region. The Sakas, Hunas, Turks, and Mughals came to India from Central Asia. Parts of India and Central Asia were ruled together during Achaemenian, Seleucid, and Kushana periods. Indian languages and scripts were in vogue in Central Asia; frescoes bearing resemblance with India's Bharut and Ajanta caves were unearthed during excavations at Penjikent in Tajikistan, Varaksha in Uzbekistan, and Azhina Tepe in Tajikistan[2].

The Sultanate and Mughal decades of Indian history (roughly from the beginning of the 13th to the early days of 18th century) witnessed the growth of caravan trade between India and Central Asia—a trade that was already established and vibrant in earlier times. This period also experienced the evolution of Indo-Islamic art and architecture, which had a very strong Central Asian imprint. The Qutab Minar in Delhi, the Taj Mahal in Agra, and Mughal miniature and Rajasthani paintings are testimonies to this cultural trend. Sufism—a crucial element in Indian Islam—has strong Central Asian connections too. Such Indian literateurs like the Hindi poet Mirza Abd al-Rahim Khan-e-Khanan or the Urdu poet Mirza Ghalib "had their roots in Central Asia."[3] The eminent Uzbek scholar Al-Beruni visited India in the 11th century and composed the celebrated treatise *Kitab-Tahkik al-Hind*. Muslim scholars, artists and soldiers, and Sufi saints from Central Asia gathered in Mughal courts. Recent studies have even demonstrated the commonalities between Uzbek and Indian musical instruments, the 'historical interrelations of the Indo-Tajik musical traditions,' and the commonness in Uzbek, Kashmiri, and Panjabi music.[4] Indian handicrafts, artisans, and builders registered their presence in Central Asia; Indian traders like Kashmiris, Peshwaris, Shikarpuris, and Punjabis were present in large numbers in Bukhara, Samarkand, and Andijan[5]. Indian masons contributed to the creation of the 'architectural treasure of Samarkand and Bukhara in Uzbekistan.[6] Amongst the Central Asian cities, Tashkent particularly had a concentration of Indian traders and teachers.[7] Many Indian cities in Gujarat are associated "with the names of Bukhari Saints and Ismaili Missionaries."[8]

Unfortunately, the intervention of British colonialism interrupted this historic link between India and Central Asia. During the Soviet regime, too, the interaction between the sub-continent and, what we now call the CIS states, was tempered through Moscow. The logistics of travel in the region had to be determined by the Soviet state agencies; Indian public sector had little presence in Central Asia, while the Indian private business was required to operate through the Soviet Foreign Travel Organisation[9]. But even within these constraints India and Uzbekistan retained a special relationship. Once the Comintern established in Tashkent the Central Asiatic Bureau of the Communist International, the city became the centre-point of anti-colonialism, including the Indian freedom movement. The Communist Party of India was itself born in Tashkent in 1920, and the first generation of India's radical nationalists and communists like M. N. Roy, Rahul Sankityayan, Abani

Mukherjee, Raja Mahendra Pratap, Sheikh Abdul Haque, and Mohammad Shafiq found a ready shelter in Tashkent. Uzbekistan was one of the four Asian republics of the former Soviet Union to participate in the Asian Relations Conference held at Delhi in March–April 1947. Our first Prime Minister Jawaharlal Nehru visited Uzbekistan twice—once in 1955, and then in 1961. Again, Tashkent was chosen in January 1966 as the venue for the peace dialogue between India and Pakistan which led to the Tashkent Declaration, although it remains a matter of deep regret that our Prime Minister Lal Bahadur Shastri breathed his last shortly after signing the Indo-Pak Declaration. The Soviet period also witnessed close cultural interactions between India and Uzbekistan. Indian film personalities like Raj Kapoor and Nargis won Uzbek hearts, and centres for studies on India developed in Uzbekistan, especially in Tashkent. The city was the centre of a series of intellectual exchanges between India and the region, figuring exchanges of teachers throughout the decades following the 1960s[10]. India opened its consulate in Tashkent in 1987. The post-Cold War period, however, opened up new possibilities of direct contacts between India and Uzbekistan, especially when the latter reoriented itself to Asia and not Russia. It is in this context that the current Indo-Uzbek relations need to be seen, and future projections require to be made.

The Present Scenario

It was certainly in the fitness of things that upon attaining her independence, Uzbekistan accorded highest priority to the sustenance and expansion of her existing warmth with India. Realising the geopolitical significance of Central Asia—lying at the crossroads of Russia, the Middle East, South Asia, and Far East—India, too, demonstrated her interest in the post-1991 era to have closer interactions with Uzbekistan. In August 1991 President Karimov chose India to undertake his first foreign visit. Since then there has been regular exchange of visits by heads of states and summit-level meetings. President Karimov visited India in 1991, 1994, 2000, and 2005. The Prime Minister Narasimha Rao went to Tashkent in 1993. On 25 and 26 April 2006 took place the historic visit to Uzbekistan of our current Prime Minister Dr. Manmohan Singh, on which occasion India reiterated the 'multi-dimensional relationship' between the two countries, and Uzbekistan stressed the 'shared view' of the two nations in multiple areas. The visit resulted in a Joint Statement stressing "the similarity or closeness of (Indo-Uzbek) positions on major regional and global issues"[11]. The latest visit to Uzbekistan by India's External Affairs Minister Shri S. M. Krishna on 22 and 23 October 2009 reaffirmed New Delhi's commitment to the historical and cultural foundations of India-Uzbekistan relationship.

India's economic linkage with Uzbekistan goes back to historical times since Uzbekistan falls in the 'crossroads' of the famous Silk Road, which connected China, India, Middle East, and Europe since the 2nd century BC. This road, provided the shortest transit route to Europe from Asia, not only promoted economic connections, but "helped the growth of human exchanges and connections for fame, fortune, and missionary pursuits which, in aggregate, promoted pluralistic traditions and cultural affinities between Central Asia and North India[12].

In the words of a leading commentator:

> "It was the most important connecting line since direct sea route from Europe to India and East Asia were yet to be discovered. Goods were not the only items that passed through these routes, the constant movement and mixing of populations also brought about the transmission of knowledge, ideas, cultures and beliefs, which had a profound impact on the culture and society of the Eurasian peoples. The trade route also facilitated the advancement of knowledge through interaction and archaeological discoveries[13]."

About 60 Indo-Uzbek Joint Agreements have been concluded till date under the auspices of which a constructive economic bilateralism exists. In 1992 the two countries signed a treaty based on "principles of interstate relations and bilateral cooperation"[14]. New Delhi offered credits worth US$ 10 million to Uzbekistan in 1992 and 1993. In 2003 the two countries concluded an Agreement on Trade and Cooperation, which continues to provide the framework of the bilateral trade. While drugs, pharmaceuticals, paper, wood products, machinery, garments and fabrics, tea, chemicals, surgical items, and consumer goods are pre-eminent in Indian exports, non-ferrous metals, machinery, silver, raw cottons, silk, pulses, and services constitute the leading items in India's imports from Uzbekistan[15]. Indo-Uzbek joint sector ventures have been also working successfully in Uzbekistan. Important amongst these are:

- Core pharmasanoat Ltd.
- Surkhan Ajantha Pharma
- Gufic Avicenna Ltd.
- Reddy Pharmed Ltd.
- Indo-Kent Plantes Ltd.
- Kaflot Kapur Fashion
- Ilyos Hotel
- Hotel Sunshine— Iuran International Ltd.
- Fashion Factory International Pvt. Ltd.
- Vinuz Ltd.
- Margilan Spun Silk Ltd.

India's public sector Bharat Heavy Electricals is involved with the power sector; such private players as Minda has invested in automobiles, the Spentex Textiles in textiles, and the Adani group in food processing[16]. In 2006 alone Spentex invested US$ 81 million. Indian participation in developmental projects in Tashkent, Bukhara, and Samarkand is substantial. Among India's new initiatives in economic bilateralism has been her supply of medical equipment worth US$ 1 million for hospitals of Uzbekistan, following the 2009 visit of India's External Affairs Minister to Tashkent[17]. More than any other Central Asian state, Uzbekistan has also unambiguously demonstrated her interest for a cooperative framework with India. The Uzbek Foreign Minister Kamilov struck the right chord, when he stressed on the occasion of the May 2000 visit of India's External Affairs Minister Jaswant Singh, the need of a 'regular and substantive contact' between the two neighbours[18].

It is, however, in the cultural sphere that the relation between India and Uzbekistan has tended to yield the most sustained results. Tashkent was the cultural centre for production of 'Asiatic Russia'. Not unnaturally, Uzbek scholars have retained an abiding interest in South Asian history and culture through Soviet days to the present times. The Institute of Oriental Studies in Tashkent has made meaningful contributions to the study of Indian languages and literature. This city's Al Beruni Institute of Oriental Studies under the Uzbek Academy of Sciences has effectively preserved its rich repository of valuable manuscripts relating to India–Central Asia relationship. Thanks to the initiative of His Excellency Professor Alquadri, the India Ambassador to Uzbekistan, the Al Beruni Institute and the University of Calcutta, India's oldest university, is being brought together through a MOU which will certainly herald a new era in deciphering the historical and multidimensional linkages between the two regions. The State Conservatoire of Uzbekistan is not only reconstructing Indo-Uzbek musical traditions, but also studying Indian languages. The Termez State University has evolved an expertise in exploring Buddhism; the Tashkent State Pedagogical University conducts researches in Indian philosophy and languages; the Fergana State University and the National University of Uzbekistan studies regional cultural, economic, and political connections.

The Uzbek interest in Indology has received reciprocation from India. The Indian Universities like Jawaharlal Nehru University and Jamia Millia Islamia, the Centre for Central Eurasian Studies of the University of Mumbai, the Centre of Central Asian Studies of the University of Kashmir, the Centre for South Central Asian Studies of Guru Nanak Dev University, the Centre for Central Asian Studies of Jiwaji University, and such institutions of higher learning like the Institute for Defence Studies, New Delhi, the Indian Council of World Affairs, New Delhi, the Indira Gandhi National Centre for Arts, New Delhi, and the Maulana Abul Kalam Azad Institute of Asian Studies, Kolkata, as well as private think-tanks like India-Central Asia Foundation continue to enrich the Central Asian Studies. Jamia Millia's course on Uzbek language has evoked enthusiastic response.

The Indian government has itself contributed to the promotion of Indian studies in Uzbekistan. On the occasion of the Prime Minister Narasimha Rao's visit to Tashkent in 1993, the Indian Cultural Centre was named the Lal Bahadur Centre for Indian Culture, and the India Chair was set up in the Tashkent University of World Economy and Diplomacy. The Indian Council of Cultural Relations offers young Uzbek scholars fellowships to pursue higher studies in India. In recent years the Government of India has also indicated its willingness to share its knowledge-base in emerging areas of science and technology. This became evident when, in the wake of Prime Minister Dr. Manmohan Singh's visit to Uzbekistan in 2006, India established with a grant of 30 million Indian Rupees the Jawaharlal Nehru India-Uzbekistan Centre for Information Technology within Tashkent's University of Information Technology. Inaugurating the Centre on 26 April 2006 in the presence of his counterpart Shavakat Mirziyayev, the India premier Dr. Manmohan Singh aptly remarked:

> "Countries must redouble efforts to bridge the knowledge gap, both within themselves and with advanced countries. It is only then that our youth and scientists can participate fully in the global market place of ideas, knowledge and information. I am confident that this Centre will train knowledge workers in Uzbekistan to enable them to compete with confidence in the global market place."[19]

We need to transform this vision into a reality. New Delhi has also offered financial assistance to set up Uzbekistan-India Entrepreneurship Development Centre in Tashkent. India is organising training programmes for Uzbek diplomats, security personnel, experts, and analysts. Uzbekistan has also recently accepted the Indian offer to "set up satellite-based tele-education and tele-medicine connectivity between the two countries[20]."

Cultural bilateralism has resulted in mutual visits of performing groups and organisation of cultural festivals. Indian singers and dancers join the colourful Sharq Taronalari music festival, held in Samarkand every two years. The 'Sogdiana' Uzbek group attracted large audience during its August–September 2004 visit to India. Uzbekistan's 'Sabo' dancing group won popular acclaim during the September 2009 Festival of Uzbek Culture in India. Similarly, the exhibition of India's musical instruments and Madhubani painting at Tashkent in 2003 was extremely popular.

Another area where Indo-Uzbek bilateralism is becoming increasingly relevant is regional and international politics. Uzbekistan has consistently advocated India's inclusion in such strategic regional groupings as the Shanghai Cooperation Organisation; she is a staunch advocate for India's permanent membership in the Security Council of the United Nations Organisation. Both countries share the common concern to create a safer world by opposing nuclear proliferation, terrorism and violence, drug trafficking, and illegal arms trade. In the words of the Uzbek President Karimov:

> "Regional problems increasingly turn into lasting sources of such dangerous threats and challenges as terrorism, violence, drug trafficking, illegal arms trade and a massive violation of human rights. These phenomena have no state boundaries[21]."

The unsettled conditions in Afghanistan, with which Uzbekistan shares a border, and the consequent spill over of terrorism from the Afghan hub have remained a common worry for India and Uzbekistan. The two countries opposed the Taliban forces in Afghanistan, and, now following the Taliban defeat, seek to have a stable Afghanistan through socio-economic reconstruction and counter Islamic fundamentalism in that area. While India has reasons to apprehend that consolidation of Islamic radicalism in Afghanistan would strengthen 'extremist pressures on Kashmir', Osama Bin Laden and other Wahabi groupings reportedly support the Islamic Movement of Uzbekistan (IMU). In 2001 the Uzbek Foreign Minister Abdulaziz Kamilov himself referred to the training of Uzbek and Tajik guerrillas in Afghan and Pakistani camps[22]. In February 1999 the Uzbek President Karimov, more than anyone else, became a target of extremists in Tashkent. A Indo-Uzbek Joint Working Group is thus working to fight terrorism in the region in all its manifestations. The two countries have also signed the Extradition Treaty as a more towards joint operations against terrorism. Uzbekistan's underlining of the importance of Indian cooperation to combat terrorism was aptly underlined by a member of the Institute of Strategic and Regional Studies of Uzbekistan:

> "India is quite experienced in handling fundamentalism and religious extremism, and since we are faced with almost identical problems, we will be glad to have the benefit of this knowledge[23]."

I just cited one example to indicate how a stable Afghanistan can help both India and Uzbekistan. According to one estimate Afghanistan exports about 75% of the world's opium[24], and 65% of the hard drugs exported from Afghanistan move through Central Asia to South Asia, and other world markets.[25] But a stable political order in Afghanistan can help both New Delhi and Tashkent to tackle this drug trafficking. Normalcy in the region would also ensure the realisation of the fruits of the proposed trans-Afghanistan transport corridor or the Zaranj-Delaram road which would considerably decrease the cost of transporting goods between India and Uzbekistan, increase the prospects of Afghanistan's integration with the regional economy[26].

The Way Forward

Recent studies propose that despite the closeness of India and Uzbekistan, the potentials of this bilateralism are yet to be realised in full. In this third section I propose to highlight some issues in this direction.

It has been suggested that Uzbekistan's rich tradition of academic and cultural linkage is essentially grounded in studying Indian language, literature, culture, and art. But it needs to be broadened based in tune with the changing geopolitical requirements. For instance, Indian and Uzbek scholars now need to draw from nation-building exercises in each other's country, and reflect how best the two countries can negotiate the challenges of the fast changing international political economy. Emphasizing this necessity, the then Indian Ambassador to Uzbekistan S. R. Tayal, while addressing an international Indology Seminar at Tashkent in March 2008, which I had the opportunity to attend, thus suggested the redesignation of Indology courses in Central Asia as Area Study Programmes[27]. We need to seriously work on that suggestion.

In their personal conversations many Uzbek scholars have also resented, and not without reason, that while Uzbekistan has enthusiastically absorbed Indian culture, the same is not perhaps true for the other way round. An entry point for addressing this imbalance is encouragement for the teaching of Uzbek language in India. A constructive Indian engagement with Uzbekistan at the policy formulation and implementation level, too, requires increasing acquaintance of the concerned Indian stakeholders with Uzbek language since the medium of instruction in Uzbekistan will increasingly tend to be Uzbek, as opposed to Russian. But it is a matter of deep regret that Jamia Millia Islamia is the only Indian university to offer a course in Uzbek. This situation should not continue. At the same time, there has to be a sizeable presence of Indian publishing houses in Uzbekistan. The Uzbek experience in the expansion of school education can be also helpful for India, as she seeks to ensure compulsory elementary school for her children under the Right to Education Act. At the same time, Uzbekistan's Gymnastics (Sports Academy) can benefit from collaboration with the Sports Authority of India. It is also imperative to point out that the Uzbek dignitaries or delegations visiting India tend to remain in and around Delhi. But they should be exposed to the periphery of the Indian federation so that the bilateral contacts become more heterogeneous and fruitful.

In the economic realm, too, there is scope of reorientation of Indo-Uzbek bilateralism. Despite a surge in Indo-Uzbek trade figures from a mere US$ 5 million in 1993-94 to US$ 116.27 million in 2008-09 and registering a 17.89% growth rate between 2007-08 and 2008-09[28], Central Asia as a region only accounts for roughly 2% of India's export trade, and only 1.5% of her import trade.[29] Uzbekistan's announcement in 2003 of current account convertibility of the local currency should, however, open new prospects from improving the trade climate with Uzbekistan, and India should take advantage of this. Another way of enhancing the Indo-Uzbek trade is to *revive* the Silk Road, but perhaps with a new orientation. This road had been a 'transit corridor', meant to cater to local markets. But if this corridor can be provided with modern infrastructure, all countries in the region are likely to benefit. For instance, the proposed Trans-Asian Highway and Trans-Asia Railway—seeking to link Europe through West and Central Asia to South, North and East Asia along the Silk Road—would enable India, especially its eastern and north-eastern part, to tap the 55 million strong Central Asian consumer market, as well the markets of southern Tibet, China, Nepal, Bhutan, Myanmar, and Bangladesh[30].

The 'New Silk Route Initiative' should also enable eastern and north-eastern India to emerge as a supplier of intermediary products and raw materials for the rapidly developing industrial units in south and south-eastern China, and other parts of South-East Asia. For example, a study has shown how the raw material produced by Haldia Petrochemicals in West Bengal for polymers and plastics can have a ready market for the expanding plastic industry in China[31]. Correspondingly, the revived Silk Road would enable the emerging economy of Uzbekistan to promote trade links with the local markets of the region. It has been also demonstrated how supply lines along the Road might held the establishment of Indo-Uzbek joint ventures[32]. Above all, the reconstruction of the Silk Road should boost tourism in the region, from which both India and Uzbekistan could derive immense economic benefit. Political stability and good neighbourly relations in the region are also likely to follow from such enhanced economic interactions.

Recent studies have even analysed how the revived Silk Route will enable India to tap the huge reserves of natural gas and oil in the Central Asian region. Central Asia has 2.7% of the total world oil reserves, and 7% of the world's total natural gas reserves. Uzbekistan itself houses the region's 74% of gas condensate, 30% of oil, 40% of natural gas, and 55% of coal. On the other hand, India is today the world's sixth largest energy consumer, experiencing a large energy deficiency, and the Indian Prime Minister Manmohan Singh has correctly noted: "energy security is second only in our scheme of things to food security"[33]. Given India's geographical proximity to Central Asia and her need to diversify the source of energy supply, Central Asian states like Uzbekistan has to feature as important source of energy. One scholar has thus aptly remarked that the Silk Route has now to be conceived as the 'Energy Route'[34]. Parallelly, India has to be involved in right earnest with such ventures as the 'energy highway' that may run from Russia via Uzbekistan, Turkmenistan and Kazakhstan to Kashmir through the India-China Line of Control. Being a land-locked country, Uzbekistan is surely to benefit from such a 'highway'. Besides, the completion of the proposed road link from Termez in Uzbekistan via Bandar Abbas and Chahbahar to Herat will reduce the current distance between Uzbekistan and India by almost 1,500 kilometres. I also feel there is enough scope of joint energy management between the 'community of energy' suppliers, represented by the Central Asian states like Uzbekistan, and the consumers represented by India. Already the Indian government has offered to train Uzbek geologists, and other experts in energy sector[35]. Possibilities of such collaborations need to be explored more.

There are other areas in which Indo-Uzbek cooperation can develop. Uzbekistan is world's second largest cotton exporter and the fifth largest raw cotton producer[36], producing between 3 to 3.5 million tonnes of cotton annually. India, with its expertise in textile technology, can readily engage itself with joint ventures in Uzbekistan in the textile sector. Indian companies can follow the model already established by Spentex and establish in Uzbekistan ginning, spinning and weaving mills based on locally available good quality cotton. Indian entrepreneurs can also cooperate with their Uzbek counterparts to set up readymade garment factories for export and local markets alike. Silk cocoon processing and commercial farming could be yet other areas of Indo-Uzbek joint ventures. Uzbekistan is now in the midst of constructing the third line for its underground Metro network. She is also poised for an expansion of her mobile telephone system. In both these areas Uzbekistan can count upon Indian expertise. Again, the computer market in Uzbekistan is largely reliant on contraband trade. But India can be an effective partner for Uzbekistan in meeting her computer requirements.

Scope exists, too, for Indo-Uzbekistan joint ventures in financial sector, small and medium scale industries for producing automatic auto components, electrical items, medical equipments like disposable syringes and blood transfusion sets, tanneries, and shoe manufacturing units.[37] Again, Uzbekistan produces considerable fruits, vegetables, meat and raw leather, but still lacks adequate processing units. India can intervene in this realm. Uzbekistan occupies the world's fifth place in gold and uranium reserves,[38] and India can not only share her skill for Uzbekistan's mineral extraction agenda, but consider Uzbekistan as an important element in the 'uranium basket' for her nuclear energy programme. Besides, Indian tea companies can think of having packaging units in Uzbekistan. Collaboration between movie industries of the two countries should be also mutually beneficial.

Possibilities exist of Indian involvement with Uzbekistan's financial sector[39]. Prospects of Indo-Uzbek industrial collaboration was evident from considerable enthusiasm generated during the India Trade Exhibition in Tashkent of 6 October 2006. On this occasion M/s. Kirloskar Brothers Ltd. donated two pump sets to Uzbekistan for installation at Samarkand[40]. It is noteworthy, unlike other CIS states, but like India, Uzbekistan has adopted a cautious approach to structural adjustment programme in the wake of globalisation.[41] This should create an added space for Indo-Uzbek cooperation. During his recent visit to Tashkent on 22 and 23 October 2009, India's External Affairs Minister Shri S. M. Krishna, even discussed the modalities of relaxing visa norms[42]. By 2009 the flow of Indian tourism to Uzbekistan had increased by 2.5 times[43], and the proposed measure should enhance the scope of tourism from both ways, given the low airfares, but, of course, with increased frequency of flights. Opening of branches of Indian banks and Indian Chambers of Commerce are also required to take advantage of new openings in economic relationship between the two countries.

Going beyond the existing contours of their relationship, India and Uzbekistan countries should identify areas of defence teamwork. Already India has established its first-ever foreign military base in Ayni in Tajikistan. There is no reason why India and Uzbekistan should not develop partnership in defence industry, particularly in the area of thermal torpedoes and other naval armaments[44]. India has already acquired from Uzbekistan the Ilyustin—78 in-flight refuelling aircraft, and Indian aircrafts are serviced at the Chkalov plant in Tashkent.[45] Such collaborations in the aviation sector could be expanded and diversified. The fact that India and Uzbekistan share a common threat perception from Pakistan and China, should be an important base for an entangled geo-strategic partnership for the two.

Conclusion

The relationship between India and Uzbekistan has to be guided both by a civilizational continuity and responses to emerging economic and geopolitical compulsions. There are sufficient potentials for a dynamic, energetic, cooperative and mutually beneficial partnership between India, the second world's fastest growing economy, and Uzbekistan, "the fulcrum around which the security of resource rich Central Asia revolves"[46]. As my submission suggests, this requires both the strengthening of existing trends and opening of new frontiers of bilateralism. In the words of a perceptible Indian commentator, who had spent two years as the India Chair at the University of World Economy and Diplomacy in Tashkent, Uzbekistan:

> "Uzbekistan is no more the copula of Russian-Indian understanding. Nor is the way of the 1990s relevant, when India had sought specific trade[47]."

India and Uzbekistan have, accordingly, to move beyond their culture driven agenda and address with a framework of cooperative bilateralism the emerging issues of international political economy and security. Although Uzbekistan's relations with many major powers have been subjected to tide and ebb, her connections with India have not only remained steady, but are expanding in multidimensional waves. India, too, has proved her commitment to, what has been aptly described as, 'all-weather friendship'[48]. For those of us who aspire for a freer and better world order, the sustenance of this friendship is of utmost importance.

As early as March 1947 Jawaharlal Nehru made a significant commented on Asian Fellowship:

> "... Asia, the mother of continents, is waking up from her old slumber. There is something of the turbulence of youth about her today and there is also something of the sparkle of youth in her eyes. An age is coming to an end and a new era is beginning for the centuries of Asia. It is fitting that on the eve of this historic change India should play hostess to the representatives of the other countries of this continent with whom she has had close and intimate relations for ages past. Those relations and contacts were cut off when India became a subject country... Now again after these centuries she is opening her doors and windows to all her neighbours and old friends ... It is a high privilege for India to inaugurate in this way this new era of Asian fellowship and comradeship in the cause of peace, freedom and progress[49]."

Nehru was speaking at the crossroad of the end of British colonialism and the rise of free India. Today, too, we are at the intersection of a new age when bipolarity is increasingly giving way to multipolarity, and in this age of transformation the Nehruvian vision of Asian Fellowship can be the guiding principle for Indo-Uzbek bilateralism, as it moves to a new constructive and challenging period of its history. It is perhaps in the same spirit that upon the assumption of his high office Prof S. M. S. Alquadri, former Indian Ambassador to Uzbekistan, remarked in his interview to *Uzbekistan Today*, [19 February 2009]:

> "Therefore, my priority as Ambassador of India is to translate our centuries-old friendly relations into a mutually beneficial economic and trade relations"[50].

Notes

1. The paper is based on a study sponsored by the Institute of Foreign Policy Studies, University of Calcutta. An initial version of the paper was presented on 27 July 2010 at the Al-Beruni Institute of Oriental Studies, Tashkent. I sincerely thank my colleagues Professor Hari Vasudevan and Dr Kingshuk Chatterjee for suggesting improvements of the essay.
2. B. B. Kumar, 'India and Central Asia: Links and Interactions'. In J. N. Roy and B. B. Kumar (eds.), *India and Central Asia: Classical to Contemporary Periods*, (New Delhi: 2007).
3. B. B. Kumar, 'India and Central Asia', p. 17.
4. Ziyadulla Nasullaev, 'Study of the Uzbek-Indian Musical Culture in the State Conservatoire of Uzbekistan'. In Jyotsna Bakshi (ed.), *Central Asia-India Dialogue: Building Partnership on the Foundation of Rich Cultural and Historical Heritage* (Tashkent: 2008).
5. Surendra Gopal, *Dialogue and Understanding: Central Asia and India: The Soviet and Post-Soviet Era* (Delhi: 2005, p. 21).
6. Evgeni Kablukov, 'India and Central Asia: Cultural Relation in Middle Ages'. In J. N. Ray and B. B. Kumar (eds.), *India and Central Asia.*
7. Ibid., p. 22.
8. M. I. Dar, 'Gujarat's Contribution to Gujari and Urdu', Islamic Culture, Vol. 27, 1953, cited in Azad N. Shamtov, 'Indo-Uzbek Literary and Linguistic Relations throughout 11-18 centuries. In Roy and Kumar (eds.).
9. Hari Vasudevan, 'India's Economic Relations with Central Asia after the "Meltdown" of 2008: A Perspective from the Trends of the Post-independence Period', *World Focus*, August 2009.

10. 'Intellectual Encounters'. In Surendra Gopal (ed.), *Dialogue and Understanding. India and Central Asia.The Soviet and Post-Soviet Era* (Shipra, New Delhi: 2005).
11. Cited in Jyotsna Bakshi, 'India and Uzbekistan: All-Weather Friendship'. In Jyotsna Bakshi (ed.) *Central Asia-India Dialogue: Building Partnership on the Foundation of Rich Cultural and Historical Heritage* (Tashkent: 2008).
12. Mustaq A. Kaw, 'Indo-Central Asian Dialogue: A Perspective on Common Cultural Affinites'. In Jyotsna Bakshi (ed.), *Central Asia-India Dialogue;* Also see, M. Kh. Abusseitova. In Jyotsna Bakshi (ed.), *Central Asia-India Dialogue.*
13. Nasir Raza Khan, 'India and the Silk Route: Problems and Prospects'. In Jyotsna Bakshi (ed.), *Central Asia-India Dialogue.* Also see Nasir Raza Khan, 'India's connection with the Silk Route', *India Quarterly*, Vol. LXI, No.1, January-March 2005.
14. See Dianne L. Smith, 'Central Asia: A New Great Game?, *Asian Affairs*, Vol.23, No.3, Fall 1996.
15. http://www.indembassy.uz/uzbekistan_econ.
16. See Hari Vasudevan, 'India's economic relations in Central Asia' and www.indianindustry.com; www.indembassy.uz/english/pmvisitindia/ipo.
17. http://www. indembassy.uz/English/news//article//33.
18. Cited in Poonam Mann, 'Fighting Terrorism: India and Central Asia', *Strategic Analysis* Vol. XXVI, No.11, February 2001.
19. http://indembassy.uz/English/pmvisitindia/jt.
20 Ministry of External Affairs, Government of India, Report, 2006, p. 43.
21. Cited in Anvar Kasimov 'On the Way to the Nuclear-Free World'. In Jyotsna Bakshi (ed.), *Central Asia-India Dialogue.*
22. Cited in Meena Singh Roy, 'India's Strategic Interests in Central Asia'.
23. Cited in Poonam Mann, 'Fighting Terrorism', p. 14.
24. 'Kazakhstan in Brief', *The Globe* (Almaty) No.13 (431), 22 February 2000, cited in ibid.
25. Nirmala Joshi's, 'Geopolitical Perspectives on Central Asia: An Indian View'. In Roy & Kumar (eds.).
26. www.indembassy.uz/english/visit/india.
27. Ambassador Tayal's Remarks in the Opening Session of the International Indology Seminar at Tashkent, 14-15 March 2008 in Jyotsna Bakshi ed. *Central Asia-India Dialogue.*
28. *Statistics of the Foreign Trade of India by Countries and Commodities*, Director General of Commercial Intelligence and Statistics, Ministry of Commerce, Government of India (Department of Commerce, Government of India, Export Import data Bank, country-wise dated 05.07.2010), http://commerce.nic.in.
29. See the Report of the Seminar on 'India-Central Asia Economic Relations' organised by Research and Information System for the Non-aligned and Other Developing Countries, New Delhi, May 2005, pp. 1-2.
30. Nasir Reza Khan, 'India's connection with the Silk Route', *India Quarterly*, Vol. LXI, No. 1, January-March 2005.
31. Ibid.

32. Ibid.
33 Quoted in Stephen Bland, 'India's energy Offensive in Central Asia', *Central Asia-Caucasus Analyst*, 9 March 2005, www.cacianalyst.org. It is felt that China has surged ahead of India in planning its energy security. See 'India Looking for Energy Supplies in Central Asia', *Asia News* 13 September 2006.
34. Nasir Raza Khan, 'India and the Silk Route'.
35. This was offered during the 7th meeting of the Uzbek-Indian Intergovernmental Commission for Trade-Economic and Scientific-Technological Cooperation held in Tashkent on 13 April 2007.
36. www.cia.gov/library/publications/the-world-factbook/geos/uz.html.
37. Gennady Chufrin, 'Partnership with India: Requirements, Possibilities and Prospects'. In Jyotsna Bakshi (ed.), *Central Asia—India Dialogue*. www.Indembassy.uz/English/Uzbekistan/econ.
38. Ibid.
39. Gennady Chufrin, 'Partnership with India: Requirements, Possibilities and Prospects'. In Jyotsna Bakshi (ed.), *Central Asia-India Dialogue*.
40. MEA Report 2006.
41. Hari Vasudevan, 'India's economic relations with Central Asia'.
42. MEA Report 2009, p. 41.
43. www.uzbekembassy.in
44. *People's Daily*, 15 November 2003, http://english.peopledaily.com.
45. Ramakant Dwivedi, 'India's Prime Minister's visit to Uzbekistan: Enhancing the Partnership', October 2006. www.uzbekembassy.in.
46. Poonam Mann, 'Fighting Terrorism'. p. 14.
47. Barun De, *Secularism at Bay: Uzbekistan at the Turn of the Century,* (New Delhi, 2006) p. 249.
48. Jyotsna Bakshi, 'India and Uzbekistan: Nurture All-Weather Friendship'. In Jyotsna Bakshi (ed.), *Central Asia-India Dialogue*.
49. Quoted in Mushirul Hasan (ed.), *Nehru's India: Select Speeches* (Delhi: 2007) pp. 105-06.
50. www.ut.uz/eng/world.